Your Free Gift

I wanted to show my appreciation that you support my work so I've put together a free gift for you.

5 Hidden Silent Secret Powers of Introverts (Bonus Gift)

Just visit the link below to access your free bonus gift.

http://www.freedomfoundationpublishing.com/introverted-

women-dating/

I know you will love this gift.

Thanks!

Jennifer C. Lowes

Contents

Introduction

Why did I write this guide?

I decided to write this guide because the majority of the books out there about dating and relationships mainly tackle one side of the equation which is Introverted Men. As an Introverted woman myself, although some of the advice for introverted men could be translated for their women counterpart, there are still some major differences between both.

There is an introvert revolution taking place in the world and I wanted to help it, contributing my grain of sand, by helping women and society in general better understand the inside world of an Introverted Woman in the Dating and Relationship arena. I believe that those who read this guide will have a competitive advantage, by learning this essential framework for Introverted Women.

Who is this guide for?

This guide is for introverted women, their partners and or anyone else who is trying to get a better understanding into the inside world of the introverted personality of a women, especially when dating or when in a relationship. If you are an Introverted Women who is starting to date again or who is already in a relationship, this guide is for you. If you are dating or in a relationship with an Introverted Women, this guide is also for you. If Introverts matter to you, then this guide should matter to you.

How to use this guide?

Each chapter of this guide can be read apart as a separate small-guide, but for the most part, it would make sense to read it all the way through, at least the first time. Then you could return to it as a reference source when required.

Chapter 1: Extraversion vs. Introversion

Extraversion and introversion is a type of classification that is done based on the different ways that people focus their attention or put their energy. Extraverts generally like to spend their time, focus and energy on the outer world – i.e. people and things. On the other hand, introverts like to spend their focus, time and energy on their inner world of ideas and imagination. At some point or other, everyone spends time either extroverting or introverting. A person is generally classified as an introvert or an extravert based on their usual characteristics.

Typical characteristics of an Extravert

>Perceived as an outgoing and a people's person

>Displays energy and enthusiasm

>Comfortable being in groups and working in groups

>Has a wide circle of friends and acquaintances

>Tendency to act first or jump into a task without thinking of the consequences

>Relaxed and confident attitude, comes across as accessible and easy to interact with

>Prefers a variety of tasks at work rather than getting too deep into an specific task

>May be perceived as shallow and pushy sometimes

>May not be as organized and planned.

>May rush to the execution part without having a full proof plan.

Typical characteristics of an Introvert

>Prefers to be alone or doing things with a few close people

>Thinks things through meticulously before acting

>Perceived as reflective or reserved

>Has fewer friends / acquaintances, usually lasting over many years

>Heavy reliance on own ideas, may not take others opinions into account

>May not be socially active or seem socially accessible

How to deal better with Extraverts

>Respond quickly in a conversation without taking too much time to think

>Maintain a free flow of communication; do not censor thoughts and ideas

>Respect the independence of extraverts

>Allow them to voice out their opinions loudly, even if it doesn't make sense

>Take the words at face value, and do not dig deeper for meaning

>Allow ample time for any discussion, getting to a conclusion may take some time

>Accept and encourage their enthusiasm in all transactions

How to deal better with Introverts

>Allow enough introduction time to make the person feel comfortable and trust you

>Respect their need for privacy from time to time

>Encourage their contribution of thoughts and ideas by creating an environment for >them to talk

>Give ample time to think and do not force or ask for opinions or ideas

>Do not embarrass them in public and only reprimand in private

>Encourage written responses wherever possible

>Do not presume quietness as a lack of interest or enthusiasm

Chapter 2: Challenges and Misconceptions – Facts and Myths about Introvert Women

The 'Introvert Woman' is usually perceived as 'different' from the 'normal' species of women that exist in our society. This species of women have some peculiar characteristics that come naturally to them, which they tend to exhibit in their daily lives. Introvert women have to constantly fight internal battles within themselves, to be able to cope with the challenges that they face in the outside world. Then there is the constant stress of being misunderstood because of their unique behavior.

Before I discuss further on the challenges that introvert women face and the consequent misunderstandings they have to deal with, I would like to announce one thing here. I am an Introvert and everyone who is like me is a normal human being like anyone else you know. We introverts are not much different from others; we just have a distinctive personality.

Every individual is different and special. To highlight this, we have tried to shed some light on the different characteristics of an introvert person in this chapter. We will discuss the misconceptions that an introvert faces, due to his/her distinctive behavior and the subsequent challenges that they face while interacting with others.

Introverts talk slow

The highlight of an introvert's behavior is that they speak slowly. That does not mean that they are mentally slow. It is just that they are not impulsive and take their time to process a certain situation before they react. They often do not find the right words in context to the discussion that they are in, since they are constantly analyzing to strike the right dialogue. It can be very frustrating and saddening for an introvert person that this is considered as a lack of intelligence by a lot of other people (read extraverts)

As an introvert, this situation needs to be dealt with lots of patience and smartness, which you know you possess, contrary to the perception of the opposite person. Since you speak slower and take your own time during a conversation, it is important that you do not try to push your opinions across just to prove to be something that you are not. This is a common perception problem that you may face anywhere, like within your home, at your workplace etc.

Introverts – A guilty bunch

Introverts spend a lot of their time feeling guilty for something that they have not done or something that they think they should be doing. Since extraverts are more in focus and receive a lot of attention, introverts are treated as a minority. This may lead to a feeling that they are not doing enough to contribute to the issues around them.

Introverts have no emotions

It would not be fair and logical to just conclude that introverts have no emotions. Every human being is emotional and has feelings towards someone or about how they feel about certain situations. Some are expressive with their feelings while others deal with their feelings from within. Introverts are the ones who will not express their emotions openly. They will rarely display their emotions in front of another person. They choose to deal with their feelings from within and due to this they are often misunderstood as curt and emotionless.

Introverts are not good public speakers

In today's world, there are many people who make their living through public speaking activities. Believe it or not, a large majority of these people are actually introverts. The inbuilt characteristics actually make them better public speakers in comparison to their counterparts.

A public speaker has a responsibility while speaking, to choose his / her words carefully considering that the people listening are motivated and guided in a particular direction. Hence, careful analysis, choice of words, thoughtful practice is of the essence for public speakers. They need to practice before delivering any speech to their audience. Incidentally, introverts fit this space perfectly since the above mentioned qualities are a part of their routine actions and a natural part of their in-built characteristics.

Introverts are shy

At social gatherings or parties introverts are considered and type casted as being 'Shy' individuals. This is absolutely a myth. Shyness is something that is got to do with low self esteem and confidence. An introvert person is often misunderstood in this context, which contributes further to the misconceptions about their attitude and characteristics. Introvert women will not interact with another person, unless they see a logical reasoning behind it.

Introverts are arrogant

Another distinctive problem and misunderstanding that introverts are faced with is that they are considered to be rude and arrogant. This is certainly not true and one should learn to appreciate when an individual chooses to be quiet or not talk much. This definitely does not mean that he / she has no opinion in the matter of discussion. Introverts are not chatter boxes, who can talk about anything under the sun. They only speak when they have something to say or something that interests them. Try starting a discussion on any topic that interests an introvert and you will be surprised to see that he / she will not stop talking.

Introverts are anti-people

Introvert people are often considered to be anti – people. This is the biggest challenge that an introvert individual faces, since we live in a society that is ready to judge a person or form an opinion on anything and everything at a drop of a pin. It is not true that introverts do not like people. The fact is when it comes to being with people, introverts like quality rather than quantity.

Introverts have a specific set of close people and they do not make unnecessary relations just to be in the thick of things. If you are friends with an introvert, then you should consider yourself privileged, as they will be your loyal ally forever. Introverts consider the fact that friendship and trust is earned and not merely a passing phase.

Introverts do not know how to have fun

Introverts are people who have a different idea of having fun. They are not the types who have an adrenaline rush to go out and do anything that comes their way. They rather opt for fun that is more tame, relaxed and peaceful. They may not enjoy a crowd, but rather a silent dinner along with their loved one in a quiet setting. They have a focused idea of fun in contrast to the others who try to find fun in everything.

Introverts are not good love partners

Every person is born with the capability to love and has the right to be loved irrespective of the nature they possess. Detailed thinking on a certain situation is an introvert individual's trait. Like discussed earlier, introverts make friends out of choice after giving it a conscious and timely thought. Naturally, they are more specific while choosing their love interests. They prove to be more loyal, caring and selfless towards their partners at all times. They are not the kinds to easily attach themselves to anyone over a casual cup of coffee.

By now, it is clear how the world perceives the image of introverts in contrast to their actual behavior. It can be safely concluded that majority of the people's perception towards introverts can certainly be altered, if not completely changed to be more adjusting and accommodating to the distinct personality of an introvert.

This will also ensure that our behavior towards introverts can be more welcoming rather than simply being judgmental. Introverts are different but equally interesting and exciting as individuals. Introverts are, in fact, a bunch of people with different shades and traits than what are commonly found in people around.

Chapter 3: Advantages of Being an Introvert Woman

It is often seen that Extraverts have it easy and have an upper hand in the society due to their exuberant, outspoken and jolly nature. However, that does not mean that the Introverts lag behind in any strata of life. It cannot be taken away from them that they too are an extremely important element of this world.

The world around us will be incomplete and different without the unique behavior and characteristics that introverts exert. The fact is the benefits of being an introvert are far more appealing. If understood well, introverts exert a far more yielding personality.

It would be unfair to say that there is a battle between extraverts and introverts in today's society. They are simply parallel tracks of a rail line, where each track is equally important to ensure that the train runs smoothly. This chapter highlights the many benefits of an introvert personality and how they are an equal force to reckon with, when it comes to their day to day lives.

Precise talkers

"Better to remain silent and thought a fool, than speak out and clear all doubt". Remaining silent during a conversation is not being foolish. An introvert has a distinct capability to gauge the topic of discussion and derive the inner meaning of it. Introverts choose their words carefully in situations, which are in turn appreciated and accepted by the group. People revere words coming from an introvert, as introverts think before talking and usually talk sense.

Creative edge

Introvert people are more creative compared to others. Creative thoughts are impulsive but the execution needs a deeper imagination. It also needs the patience to chalk out the plan, considering the feasibility of the project. This is an apt situation for introvert personalities, since they have a character of embracing wise thoughts. They have a great sense of focus with extended time durations of concentration, which is essential to complete any task and to get the desired results.

Good listeners

"If all speak, who will listen?" There is no need to think twice as to who the listeners are in this case. Introverts naturally come across as exceptional listeners who often cater to matters where important decisions are to be made. Who wouldn't like to have a good friend who will patiently hear out your problems? The introvert is an ideal friend one can have, since many of our issues just need a non judgmental ear. This helps in reducing stress, as speaking out about issues without being judged, helps.

Socially responsible

Since introverts are calm and silent they are more appreciated and loved. Introverts are unlike the head bangers or the loud mouths that create nuisance and discomfort, to people around, for the sake of their enjoyment and thrills.

Their peculiar sense of observation and sensitivity towards their surroundings makes them ideal candidates as tenants. People look forward to welcoming introvert personalities into their homes rather than a boisterous lot.

Self-reflective

We have read and heard often that the best thing one could do to himself / herself is to self introspect in order to get the answers from within, which are always right. This is one trait that most people have to adapt but fail to do so in their busy lives. Introspection comes naturally to introverts, which is an enviable quality they possess.

They have the ability to look within and find inner peace, which everyone seems to be running around searching for elsewhere. They invest a lot of time introspecting, which eventually helps them connect with their inner mind and soul. Due to this, they have a better understanding of their own self.

Zealous experts

There are experts and then there are zealous experts. Introverts are zealous experts for the sheer determination, inner energy, passion and time they invest in the things that they do. It may sound easy to comply with each of the above attributes, but in fact it might be a challenge for other people. Introverts naturally exhibit these characteristics within their personality. A deep understanding and valuable analysis of issues, make introverts a class apart.

Balanced lifestyle

Introverts are precise talkers, having a creative edge over others in their thoughts. They are also socially responsible at the same time. These are perfect qualities that one would associate with a person who leads a balanced life. Introverts are soon gaining the reputation of people who have the most balanced lifestyle in every aspect. The credit for this totally goes to their controlled nature. Introverts are not parasites that thrive on other elements to complete their life. They are self-equipped to pick themselves up in any situation and rely on their own judgment.

Chapter 4: Famous Introvert Women

After going through the above chapters, we are clear in our head that we need some middle ground – we need to appreciate and respect both extravert and introvert female personalities for all their contributions to business, academia, personal relationships et al.

It is wrong in this case to champion a one-sided image of a successful woman – one that is extraverted and hence supposedly a role model for strength and leadership. If we do this, then not only are we not appreciating the qualities of an introvert woman, we are also pushing her more and more to ape the behaviors of an extravert woman. This is completely unnatural to her and may not add any value to either herself or the environment around her.

To dispel the myth that introverted women cannot be successful, we have listed below a few of the famous (introvert) women personalities who have proved the above adage wrong.

Audrey Hepburn

Audrey Hepburn continues to rule our hearts and is an amazing role model for women all over even after her death in 1993. She has been, in fact quoted as saying, "I'm an introvert...I love being by myself, love being outdoors, love taking a long walk with my dogs and looking at the trees, flowers, the sky". She has not just been a very talented and successful actress, but also served as a UNICEF Goodwill Ambassador. She tirelessly worked and spoke for the betterment of underprivileged children, despite her introverted nature.

J K Rowling

The super successful author of the Harry Potter series needs no introduction. However, just as most successful writers need to be strong introverts, spending maximum time alone, in front of a computer or a book, she too is a self proclaimed introvert. She was so attuned with her thoughts and ideas that she created an entire wizarding world in a short span of 4 hours, in a train journey!

Christina Aguilera

This pop star and TV reality judge might seem like a perfect picture of an extravert person on screen and on stage; however, in reality, she identifies herself as an intense and introverted woman. She has always maintained that she's felt like an 'outsider' her entire life. Yet, she hasn't let that ever come in her way, whether it be displaying her craft as a total exhibitionist, or even winning four Grammys in the process.

Eleanor Roosevelt

Eleanor Roosevelt is the longest serving First Lady in American history and is famous and well known for her well rounded persona. She is known for her charity work, contributing at major discussion forums, holding press conferences and also serving as an American spokesperson in the United Nations after her husband's death. However, she was also known to be an introvert by nature, often described as a shy and awkward child who grew up into a woman with a lot of sensitivity towards the needs of the underprivileged.

Her gracious and purposeful nature endeared her to many and made her an effective spokesperson for the world during the World War II. Often, she has been quoted as saying, "Friendship with oneself is all important, because without it one cannot be friends with anyone else in the world."

Emma Watson

Emma Watson, the lovable actress from the Harry Potter series and movies like – 'The perks of being a wallflower', is known as a non-party girl and an introvert. She has been quoted as saying, "It's interesting, because people say things to me like, 'It's really cool that you don't go out and get drunk all the time and go to clubs,' and I'm just like, I mean, I appreciate that, but I'm kind of an introverted kind of person just by nature, it's not like a conscious choice that I'm making necessarily. It's genuinely who I am"

Although she has been made to realize time and again that something is 'different' about her and lacking because she is not an extravert, she has taken that knowledge in her stride. She used it to empower herself about her natural strengths and abilities from being an introvert. She is in fact super successful, as the highest grossing actress of the past decade.

Marissa Mayer

Marissa Mayer, the 38 year old Yahoo! President and CEO is known to be naturally shy and introverted by nature. However, that does not stop her from being a dynamic business leader, extracting best performance from her peers, making important business decisions for the company and improving business through her thought leadership and creativity, all strengths of an introverted person. Nevertheless, the media always showcases her to be extravert by nature, since there is a general misconception that only extraverts make effective leaders.

Courtney Cox

The former actress from the super successful 'Friends' TV show, is a self proclaimed 'homebody' and introvert. In her words she likes to socialize by having a few people over at home. This was also cited as a reason for her split with her ex-husband, David Arquette, who is an extraverted personality and quite the opposite.

Laura Bush

The former First Lady and wife of President George W. Bush is also a self described introvert. She has also claimed that she and her husband are completely opposite in nature. However, she is a perfect example of the fact that being an introvert doesn't mean being a shy person. She has always come across as confident, humorous and purposeful in all her talks and public addresses. She also has a way with the press, also turning down the theory that the press has about her being shy, remote and politically ill informed.

Chapter 5: Dating Tips & Tricks for Introvert Women

By now, we know that introvert women are different and special. At the same time they have some tremendous inner power in the way they conduct and manage their lives. Love is a part of it and they are no different when it comes to this subject. Their analyzing and intimate selective nature makes them a class apart when it comes to dating. Many introvert women are not sure of the approach, though they are sure of the opposite person.

This chapter sheds some light on some tips and tricks introverts can adopt while dating.

Do not bluff

The thumb rule for any women who is going on a date irrespective of the nature or personality is not to 'Bluff'. Do not pretend to be someone that you are not. It is absolutely fine to be an introvert and you should love yourself for who you are. Irrespective of whether you are really interested in the person or not, it is best to present the actual you to the opposite person. Not to forget, men like mysterious women.

Comfort zone

As an introvert, your comfort zone is an essential decisive factor when you go out on a date. Keeping this in mind, choose a location to your comfort, preferably a place that you have already visited and are comfortable with. Avoid noisy and loud places since such venues may put you on edge and make you uncomfortable and may not interest you.

Take advice

Taking advice is always a wise option at all times. The same applies to the rules of dating. You can consult another introvert friend or family member who has gone through a similar experience. The situation might not necessarily be the same, but the advice on the strategy and approach will certainly help. You can even look up for advice on the internet or through self-help strategies.

Take small steps

As an introvert woman, you need to take one step at a time. Since that is a highlight of your inner personality, it is advisable to keep your first date prompt and crisp. It may be hard for you to mingle easily with people and be social, so a small meeting at a coffee shop should be just the perfect start.

Ask questions

Analysis and clear and precise knowledge of a situation or person is an introvert's hallmark need. Hence, ask questions to your date that will help you know him better and also help you take a decision as to where the date is heading.

Keep the alcohol trip short

If you decide to drink on your date, it is recommended that you do not binge. Alcohol has proven to be a good catalyst to ease down a situation and to create a more social environment. But at the same time, there is a fine line between social drinking and creating a social nuisance. So keep a firm count on how much you drink. A couple of drinks are safe and something you should stick to, especially on your first date.

Search for similarities

No two individuals are exactly the same. This does not mean that two people cannot have similar likes, dislikes or hobbies. On your date take up the initiative to find similarities between you and your date. Alternatively, you could also look up for a partner online, with choices and interests that are similar to yours. This will help you find the potential and desirable friend or companion.

Online dating

This point is in continuation to the previous one. In todays technological and internet space, the world has become smaller and is bringing people closer. Online dating is an exceptional medium for introverts, since one is not directly facing the opposite person. Expressing one's feelings indirectly through an online medium becomes much easier and this is what best suits an introvert personality too. So the comfort zone is automatically created wherein an introvert person can interact with potential partners and seek a great way to start a relationship before you actually meet up and take it forward from there. But beware of creepy men, who are abundant on such online dating sites.

Being mysterious is fine

Mystery and suspense has always been a thrill whether people accept it or not. If you are an introvert woman, take it as your scoring point. It is perfectly fine if the person you are dating feels that you do not talk much and are a mystery that they need to slowly unravel and understand. This will not only make your date more inquisitive and interested in you, but also develop a need to get to know you better by meeting you again and more often.

Do not be the passenger seat rider

If your date is an outright extravert, there is a possibility you will be a push over in the relationship, whether you like it or not. You will not realize what exactly is happening since the stronger personality is taking charge of you and also of the situation all the while. It is only after a few days that it sinks in as to which boat you are sailing in. To avoid this, take subtle charge of the date right from the start. Learn to say 'NO' if something is not fine with you. Be clear with your date that you'd like to take things a little slower if you are uncomfortable of the speed at which things are moving.

Avoid the numbers game

Often, you might feel that you are lagging behind in regards to the conquests that your friends have achieved with men. Here we imply the number of men that they've dated or even the type of men that they have dated. Remember it is quality for you and not necessarily the quantity. So there is no reason why you should fall prey to top the numbers game. Take your time, go with the flow, and if you sincerely feel that the date is right for you, go for it.

Generate the right vibes

No matter what anyone's opinion is about love at first sight, sight is the first step towards attraction and the rest follows later. It is of prime essence that you display the right vibes if you want to send out positive signals. Hence, your dressing and body language has to compliment your mind set when you are looking for a date and when you are in a social place. Make a conscious effort to exuberate the right stance and personality when you are in a group. Being an introvert definitely does not mean that you cannot give out the right signal. Be confident of yourself, people will love you for who you are.

Dating has always been a task irrespective of gender or personality. If one gets the simple steps right and sticks to the basics, it should lead to a wonderful time that one can spend with their partner. A date may eventually result in a long term relationship, once both the partners have got to know each other. Simple understanding and learning about each other's common interests and accepting one another's differences can go a long way in contributing to the success of a relationship.

Chapter 6: Socializing Tools for an Introvert Woman

An introvert woman is widely thought of as a loner, anti social and a closed personality. But by now, it is crystal clear that it is absolutely not true and just a myth. But as introverts, we need to take on the responsibility to clear this misconception and make others realize that we are just like any one of them.

This chapter captures some simple, everyday tips and tricks for the introvert women, to help them come out of their shell and be more acceptable and understood within their social circle.

Let yourself to be social

The primary and vital tool for socializing is to be prepared from within to go out and approach people. It may seem like a challenge to do so, as it is a shift from what you are used to do, or a shift from your usual comfort zone. You might not be an out and out people's person, but you certainly need to interact at various stages in your life and make an effort to build relationships with people around you. Prepare and allow yourself from within to take this all important step towards networking or connecting in society.

Understand yourself

Introvert women are known for their slow pace in opening up, especially at social gatherings or social places. It is quite essential that as an introvert you are sensitive towards your own feelings and emotions. In turn, you need to attune them to help you display a favorable personality to others while at social gatherings. This will enable people to understand you better and also endear you to others, thus winning half the battle for you.

Start slow

Socializing and networking does not come to you naturally, so do not run before you learn to walk. Take it easy and slow when you begin this journey. It is advisable to start socializing with a few people that you are close to or feel most comfortable with, slowly gain confidence from experiences and then spread your wings. It is easier to focus on a smaller number at the beginning to make the conversations more specific and simpler to handle.

Get help from an extravert

An introvert is gifted with a talent to listen to people and understand situations better. If you have a friend/s who is an extravert, it would only be wise to listen and assimilate from them what is expected from you. This is a much faster and effective way of learning and you will find yourself well equipped before you get social with a larger group of people.

Choose your own field

Introverts do exceptionally well when they are in their zone or field of expertise. They understand the complexity of the particular situation, as well as the people involved in it. When you start the networking path, remember to choose people having similar preferences, hobbies or interests. This will give you a jump start in gaining confidence and speaking out with more comfort and confidence because you know the rules of the game.

Avoid Favoritism

As an introvert we naturally get deeply attached and involved to people we emotionally connect with. But the larger picture has a little different set of rules. While socializing we interact with different people and each individual needs to be respected and acknowledged during a conversation. Hence, favoring a particular person/s might just push you on to the back seat and make you appear as though you practice favoritism. Being neutral and equally open to everyone in a group by being 'inclusive' in conversations, you will score brownie points with everybody.

Always carry a smile

"Smiles win hearts" is a proven adage, especially when it applies to a woman. Irrespective of the location or the type of people, carry a smile on your face when interacting with people face to face. It is the first step that sends a message across that you welcome the interaction and that you would genuinely like to get to know the opposite person better. It gives the person on the receiving end a reason to smile back at you too and in many cases, it is the simplest and most effect way of breaking the ice and starting a conversation.

Keep questions open ended

A social gathering does not always mean a 'Party'. You may be at an informal meet up with colleagues or places where you need to interact with people. Always keep your questions open ended. Avoid taking the lead right away. Asking too many questions right away will project you as an interrogation officer. You can take the role of a listener. Every gathering needs a good listener as well.

Chapter 7: Some Dos and Don'ts While Dating an Introverted Woman

After going through the above chapters, we can learn and appreciate the fact that introvert women are more focused, loyal and interesting, once you get to know them. They appear to be low on confidence initially, but once you get to know them, you understand that they are much more confident and purposeful than what their outer appearance suggests.

In the previous chapter, we have shared some dating and socializing tips and tricks and how to manage an exciting dating life if you are an introvert woman / from the point of an introvert. However, in this chapter, we tackle an equally important subject – what if you are an extravert by nature and your partner is an introvert. This means that you are two conflicting personalities in a relationship trying to make it work.

As such, you will need a bit of an understanding and patience with your introvert partner and certain tips and tricks to ensure that you do not rub an introvert the wrong way. The idea is to keep the flame burning and make the relationship work. We have highlighted some suggestions to help you with the same in this chapter.

Flirting

It is easier flirting with an introvert partner because you can be sure than once you have their attention; they will focus just on you. Unlike people with extravert personalities, whose attention may waver hunting for the next target soon enough, introverts are usually focused on their partners.

However, a pitfall can be that the onus of initiating the action may fall on you every time. Considering you are an extrovert, it is no big deal for you. You can slowly try and show your interest by smiling, through your body language and also through your eyes. Then you can slowly initiate a dialogue with your potential partner.

Be careful of not being too pushy once you initiate things, let your introvert partner ease into the game. If there is absolutely no response, don't push too much and move on.

Places to go

Avoid taking your introvert date to places where you fear that she could become the centre of attention. Most introverts hate being in such places. Avoid places like karaoke where your date could be expected to sing or a comedy club where your date might be picked out of a crowd or book clubs where you might be expected to contribute your thoughts.

Instead take them to a pub or a comfortable place with a live band or a dinner buffet where there is no chance of them being singled out for attention.

Conversation

You will need to understand the fact that you may have to take the initiative to start conversations and be the one doing most of the talking. Well, it doesn't mean that you have to keep on blabbering and talk for the heck of speaking.

Introverts are measured by their conversations and do not indulge in small cheesy talks. They will only talk about a few things that are personally important to them. At such times, you need to give a careful listening ear to be able to understand them. Introverts appreciate a good listener, who would let them talk only as much as they are comfortable with and who does not pressurize them into talking incessantly.

However, be aware if your date is just on the 'quiet side' or being completely silent. Complete silence could also indicate a lack of interest and you would not want to waste further time trying to draw that person out into a conversation.

Keeping in touch

Once you have been out on a date or multiple dates with your introvert partner and are trying to be in touch through the phone, do not get discouraged if you do not get an enthusiastic response. It is most likely that if the call is not important or urgent they will let it go into voicemail a lot of times.

To avoid any disappointment, it is better to have a texting plan ready instead, as introverts do not feel threatened to text back. Talking may make them feel like being in a spot, whereas, they may not feel conscious when texting. They may even open up in a better manner on text. This way you can be sure that they will say what they want to say and you will also get a good glimpse into their true feelings.

Communication

When you spend time with an introvert, you will realize that your style of communication is very different from your partner's style of communication. An introvert partner may be a reluctant communicator, preferring a few words and short conversations / messages / emails.

However, this might be a little frustrating if your partner does not communicate with you when you need it, and in the way and style that you look forward to. If you are able to adjust to a little bit of mystery and understand that reluctance in communication is not lack of feelings / interest, then you can pull on with your partner.

But if you feel it is really challenging, and leads to a serious doubt of the person's interest levels in you, then it might be time to have a frank chat with your partner. If things do not improve, then consider it as a time to move on.

Socializing

It is almost a ground rule while dating an introvert partner that you do not take them to parties and abandon them alone. Firstly, avoid taking them to parties where you know a lot of people but they don't, as they will soon enough feel left out and uncomfortable. Even if there are other common acquaintances, it is advised that you don't leave your date alone to fend for themselves, as this is inexcusable.

Stay close to them! If you are taking them to work parties, make it a point to introduce them to your work mates and colleagues and help them to introduce themselves in case they find it uncomfortable. Ensure you spend enough time together, even in crowded parties to make it a good experience for them.

Fights and Conflicts

If you get through the initial stages of dating an introvert and are in an active relationship, chances are you will be faced with fights and conflicts just like in any other relationship. However, the unique thing here is the way the two personalities differ when approaching and resolving a conflict.

Rest assured that an introvert, while responding to a conflict, will be very slow but very thoughtful and will never be brash and/or thoughtless. As such, you can always hope to have a sensible and practical argument with an introvert. On the other hand, if you are looking for instant closure, it might be a bit frustrating as conflict resolutions tend to get delayed due to their introverted nature. They take time in responding, thus may bring up the issue, maybe a few days later.

Be sure to resolve the conflicts when they arise; if not immediately, then as and when comfortable to both, to avoid any build up of resentment and distrust. Be as understanding and flexible as possible, while at the same time making realistic expectations with your partner.

Practicing Silence

Don't try to talk every time or fill every moment of silence with some conversation when you are with your introvert partner. Initially long period of silences might be a bit awkward; however, you need to understand that expecting small and meaningless talk from introverts just to fill in the silence is a little unrealistic. It is best if you avoid doing that as much as you can. Instead, accept quality over quantity and indulge in some thoughtful conversations on topics that might interest her. Do common activities together, which does not require much of talking but also bring you both closer to each other.

Chapter 8: How to make an Introvert – Extravert Relationship Work

Introverts and Extraverts have opposite ways of dealing with stressful situations and meeting their emotional needs. Introverts seek more time with their own self and their inner thoughts from time to time in order to re-fuel themselves. On the other hand, extraverts seek the companionship of people and the external world in order to find answers to their questions and to re-fuel themselves.

Hence, it might seem a bit countering / conflicting to suggest that these two opposite personality types should get together in a relationship, but it actually makes complete sense. Two extraverts paired together run the risk of burning themselves out without sufficient time for any rest or self-reflection. Whereas, on the other hand, two introverts together would mean insufficient external stimuli and a general feeling of two people living on an island cut off from the outside world, which is again not good for personal and relationship growth.

This does not mean that same personality alliances necessarily do not work or are doomed. It is important to understand that each relationship has its unique challenges and that it is important to find the right balance from time to time. Each partner should not feel, at any time, that his/her needs are repeatedly being ignored or compromised in the process. It is important to not be judgmental about the opposite person's personality and instead be grateful of the value that your differences bring to your relationship, making it more complementary and wholesome.

In this chapter, we focus on an introvert - extravert relationship and how you can make things work in a better and smoother fashion. These include some practical guidelines and tips and tricks that you could practice in your day to day lives:

Clearly define your needs

Instead of just saying what you feel like doing and then inviting arguments and fights and disagreements, be sure that you clearly mention your reasons and objectives for wanting to do something.

It is very likely that your reasons behind wanting to do certain things or activities may not be in agreement with what your partner wants to do. At such times, if your reasons are clearly known to your partner, it will ensure that they are more agreeable and acceptable towards your needs.

Adjust to each other's social needs

Always ensure that you introduce your partner in parties or social gatherings. Having lots of people around may throw an introvert person into an acutely uncomfortable situation. Whereas having a close, intimate party might run the risk of getting boring and predictable for an extravert person. Hence, it is important to plan carefully and in this case take your introvert partner's needs as priority and adjust a bit to them.

Setting limits and boundaries

Having good knowledge about what is a 'maybe' and what is a 'complete no-no' with your partner and then being sensitive towards the same, will go a long way in ensuring a smooth relationship. There will be circumstances that may be acceptable to your partner or that he / she is willing to adjust for you. This is as far as how much you can push your boundaries. This will also enable you to find the most valuable 'middle ground' to carry on a healthy relationship.

Making friendships

If you are the extravert in an introvert-extravert relationship, it is very likely that you come with a large group of friends circle or acquaintances, most of whom your introvert partner does not get along with. This will always make you both fall into a vicious cycle with the extravert pulling the introvert into social engagements and parties that the introvert is uncomfortable in.

He/ She may eventually start avoiding social engagements, leading to disengagement, bitterness and fights. It is very advisable that while you both maintain your old friendships one-on-one, both of you develop and forge new friendships together within a few months of the relationship so that you move on with your stages of friendship, cohesively and together.

Respecting compromises

There will be times when each partner will compromise his / her own joy or comfort or needs for the happiness of the other like going to a social event, attending a meeting, or even other hobbies or activities that may not particularly be of interest to one. In such situations, the other partner must learn to appreciate and comfort the compromises and sacrifices of the other, and ensure that the channels of communication are always open, thus, nurturing and making the relationship stronger without making the other person feel left out.

Spending quality time together

One-on-one time is sacred to any relationship and helps in building and strengthening a relationship like nothing else. However, in the case of an introvert-extravert relationship, spending special time alone might connote different meanings. It is very important to take both point of views into consideration and arrive at some compromise or understanding. Some days can be dedicated to doing activities that one partner enjoys and on other days doing something that the other partner enjoys, thus achieving equitable ground.

Finding the right balance

As highlighted earlier, not just an introvert-extravert relationship, but any kind of relationship might be full of compromises and adjustments. However, finding the right balance, setting the right expectations, and constant love and understanding can go a long way in making these compromises work for your relationship and not go waste. The couple should not feel bitter while compromising, or feel that the compromises are one-sided always. This is the key to finding the right balance.

Your Free Gift

I wanted to show my appreciation that you support my work so I've put together a free gift for you.

5 Hidden Silent Secret Powers of Introverts (Bonus Gift)

Just visit the link below to access your free bonus gift.

http://www.freedomfoundationpublishing.com/introverted-women-dating/

I know you will love this gift.

Thanks!

Jennifer C. Lowes

www.ingramcontent.com/pod-product-compliance
Lightning Source LLC
Chambersburg PA
CBHW070239290526
45789CB00004B/1689